Maths Revision
for CCEA GCSE 2-tier s[pecification]

T6

Compiled by Patrick McGurk

Contents

1a Non-calculator 3

2a With calculator 9

1b Non-calculator 14

2b With calculator 21

Answers 27

Approved/endorsed by CCEA on 30 April 2012. If in any doubt about the continuing currency of CCEA endorsement, please contact CCEA. Whilst the publisher has taken all reasonable care in the preparation of this book CCEA makes no representation, express or implied, with regard to the accuracy of the information contained in this book. CCEA does not accept any legal responsibility or liability for any errors or omissions from the book or the consequences thereof.

Publisher's Note
This book has been written to help students preparing for the GCSE Mathematics 2-tier specification from CCEA. While Colourpoint Books and the authors have taken every care in its production, we are not able to guarantee that the book is completely error-free. Additionally, while the book has been written to closely match the CCEA specification, it the responsibility of each candidate to satisfy themselves that they have fully met the requirements of the CCEA specification prior to sitting an exam set by that body. For this reason, and because specifications change with time, we strongly advise every candidate to avail of a qualified teacher and to check the contents of the most recent specification for themselves prior to the exam. Colourpoint Books therefore cannot be held responsible for any errors or omissions in this book or any consequences thereof.

Maths Revision Booklet T6

Revision Exercise 1a   (non-calculator)

You must **not** use a calculator for this paper. Total mark for this paper is 50.
Figures in brackets printed down the right-hand side of pages indicate the marks awarded to each question or part question.
You should have a ruler, compasses, set-square and protractor.

1

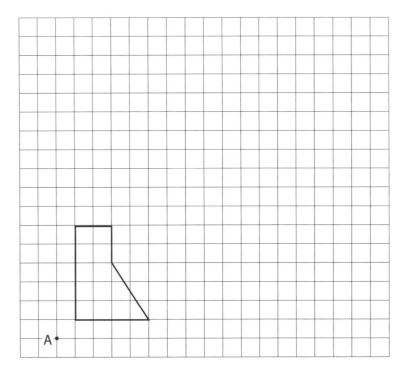

Enlarge the shape by a scale factor 2 about the point A.   [3]

2 (a) Find the value of R when S = −12 and T = −8

$$R = \frac{6(S - T)}{2}$$

Answer R = _____ [3]

(b) Calculate the value of s in the formula below where u = 40, a = −5 and t = 3

$$s = ut + \tfrac{1}{2}at^2$$

Answer s = _____ [2]

3 Estimate the value of

$$\frac{509 \times 6}{(89.3 + 58.9)}$$

Answer _____ [2]

4 A tin contains chocolate, nut, fruit and mint sweets. The probabilities of selecting each type of sweet at random from the tin are shown in the table below.

Type	Chocolate	Nut	Fruit	Mint
Probability	0.25	0.2	0.4	

(a) What is the probability of selecting a mint sweet?

Answer _____ [2]

(b) What is the probability of **not** selecting a chocolate sweet?

Answer _____ [2]

The tin contains 240 sweets.
(c) How many fruit sweets are there in the tin?

Answer _____ [2]

5 (a) Simplify $\dfrac{a^3 \times a^6}{a^2}$

Answer _____ [1]

(b) Calculate the reciprocal of 0.6

Answer _____ [2]

6 A and B are two points which are 12 cm apart. By shading, find the locus of points which are less than 7 cm from A and such that the distance from A is greater than the distance from B.

[3]

7 l, r and h are lengths.
Write down whether each of the following formulae represents length, area, volume or none of these.

(a) $5\pi r^2 + \pi r l$

Answer _____ [1]

(b) $6\pi r^2 h + \pi r \sqrt{(r^4 + h^4)}$

Answer _____ [1]

8 (a) Complete the table below for $y = 2x^2 - 6x - 5$ for values of x from -2 to 5.

x	-2	-1	0	1	2	3	4	5
y	15		-5	-9		-5	3	15

[2]

(b) Draw the graph of $y = 2x^2 - 6x - 5$ for values of x from $x = -2$ to $x = 5$

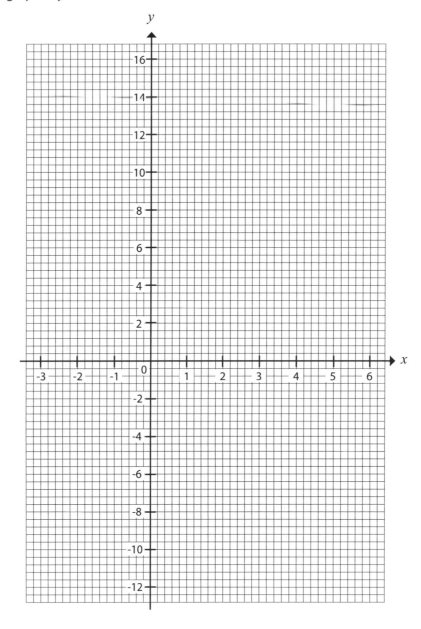

[2]

(c) Draw the line $y = -3$ and find the x values of the points of intersection of the line with $y = 2x^2 - 6x - 5$

Answer $x =$ _____ and $x =$ _____ [2]

(d) Write down the equation in x with the solutions found in part **(c)** and simplify it.

Answer _____ [1]

9 (a) Simplify $(\sqrt{5})^2$

Answer _____ [1]

(b) Express $\frac{4}{11}$ as a recurring decimal

Answer _____ [1]

(c) Rationalise the denominator of $\frac{5}{2\sqrt{3}}$

Answer _____ [2]

(d) Given $y^3 = \frac{20}{6x^2}$ and $y = 10$, find x in the form $a\sqrt{b}$

Answer _____ [3]

10 (a) Simplify the expression $(3x^2y^3z^4)^2$

Answer _____ [2]

(b) Rearrange the expression to make c the subject

$$t = \frac{cy + s}{cx}$$

Answer _____ [3]

(c) simplify $(5 + 2\sqrt{10})^2$

Answer _____ [2]

11 (a) In triangle ABC, AB = h and BC = R
In triangle ADE, AD = x and DE = r

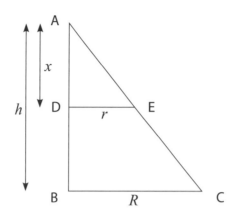

By using the method of similar triangles, show that $x = \dfrac{rh}{R}$

[2]

(b) A frustum is formed from a cone with a circular base radius R and height h by cutting off the tip of the cone with a cut perpendicular to the height, forming a lower base and an upper base which are circular and parallel. The radius of the tip of the cone is r and its perpendicular height is x.

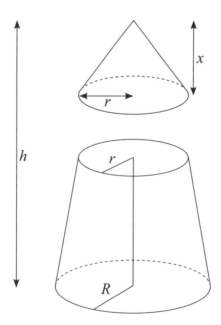

Using the information in part (a), show that the volume V of the frustum is given by $V = \dfrac{\pi h}{3R}(R^3 - r^3)$

[3]

Maths Revision Booklet T6

Revision Exercise 2a   (with calculator)

You may use a calculator for this paper. Total mark for this paper is 50.
Figures in brackets printed down the right-hand side of pages indicate the marks awarded to each question or part question.
You should have a ruler, compasses, set-square and protractor.

1 (a) Which of "always even", "always odd", "could be odd or even" describes the number $n^2 + 1$ where n is an odd number. Explain.

Answer _____

_____ [2]

(b) "The sum of two prime numbers is always even." Give an example which proves this statement wrong.

Answer _____ [1]

2 The recipe needed to make an energising sports drink is

 Orange juice   100 ml
 Sugar   56 g
 Salt   12 g
 Water   1900 ml

(a) John makes some of the sports drink. He uses 25 ml of orange juice. How much salt does he use?

Answer _____ g [1]

(b) Sheila uses 84 g of sugar to make the sports drink. Find the amounts of orange juice, salt and water used.

orange juice _____ ml
salt _____ g
water _____ ml
[3]

3 Michael works in the Civil Service and earns an annual salary of £31000
The amount of tax which Michael pays is calculated from the taxable bands and the rates of tax shown in the table below.

Tax Bands	Tax rate
Personal allowance up to £5435	0%
£0 – £2230 taxable income	10%
£2231 – £34600 taxable income	22%

Calculate the annual amount of tax that Michael pays.

Answer £ _____ [3]

4

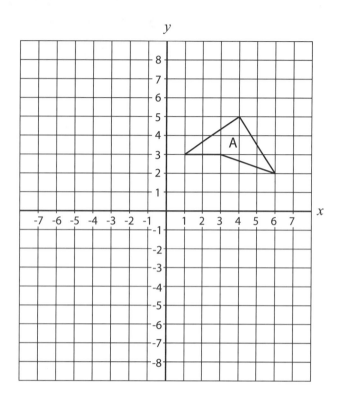

(a) Reflect shape A in the y axis. Label the reflection B. [1]

(b) Reflect shape B in the x axis. Label this reflection C. [1]

(c) Reflect B in the line $y = x$. Label this reflection D. [2]

(d) Describe fully the single transformation which maps A onto C.

Answer _____

_____ [3]

5

The graph represents Mr Brown's journey from Belfast to Donegal town. Mr Brown stopped for a break at a service station outside Dungannon.

(a) For how long did Mr Brown stop?

Answer _____ minutes [1]

Mr Brown resumed his journey but had to slow down outside Enniskillen because of heavy traffic.

(b) For how many miles did he travel at a slower average speed?

Answer _____ miles [1]

Mr Brown arrives in Donegal town at 12 noon. He attends a meeting for 40 minutes and returns non stop to Belfast at an average speed of 50 miles per hour.

(c) Complete the travel graph for Mr Brown's journey. [2]

Mr Green leaves Belfast at 9.30am and drives directly to Donegal town at an average speed of 45 miles per hour.

(d) Draw the line showing Mr Green's journey. [2]

(e) How far apart were Mr Brown and Mr Green at 9.50am?

Answer _____ miles [2]

(f) At what time did Mr Green overtake Mr Brown?

Answer _____ [2]

(g) How far were Mr Brown and Mr Green from Donegal town when Mr Green passed Mr Brown?

Answer _____ miles [1]

6 The density of beech wood is 740 kg/m³. Calculate the mass of a block of beech which has a cross-section area of 0.19 m² and length 7.1 m. Give your answer to an **appropriate degree of accuracy**.

Answer _____ kg [3]

7 200 boys and 300 girls were asked to select their choice of fruit from an apple and an orange. The probability of a boy choosing an apple was $\frac{3}{5}$ and the probability of a girl choosing an apple was $\frac{3}{4}$. How many boys and girls chose an apple?

Answer _____ [3]

8 n is a number written in standard form.
When n is multiplied by 8.6×10^6, the result is 4.902×10^{11}.
Find n.

Answer $n =$ _____ [2]

9 A hat contains 6 red balls and 4 blue balls.
Two balls are selected at random from the hat. The first ball is selected at random and is not replaced. A second ball is then selected from the hat.

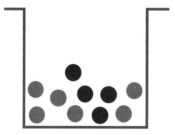

(a) Complete the probability tree diagram below to show the probabilities.

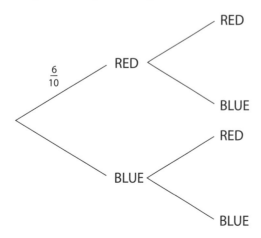

[2]

(b) What is the probability of selecting two blue balls?

Answer _____ [1]

(c) What is the probability of selecting at least one red ball?

Answer _____ [2]

10

A right circular closed cone has a base radius of 10 cm and slant height 26 cm. Find the total surface area.

Answer _____ cm² [2]

11 A first year pharmacy student has to sit 3 examinations in 'Microbiology', 'Biochemistry' and 'Ethics and Practice'.
In Microbiology, the probability of her passing the examination is $\frac{8}{10}$
In Biochemistry, the probability of her passing the examination is $\frac{7}{10}$
In Ethics and Practice, the probability of her passing the examination is $\frac{9}{10}$

Assuming that the probability of the student passing any examination is independent of each of the other examinations, use a tree diagram or otherwise to calculate the probability that:
(a) (i) she will pass all three papers

Answer _____ [2]

(ii) she will fail all three papers

Answer _____ [2]

(iii) she will pass at least one of the papers

Answer _____ [2]

The student needs to pass at least two of the three examinations to proceed into the second year of her studies.
(b) Calculate the probability that she will succeed in going into the second year course.

Answer _____ [2]

Revision Exercise 1b (non-calculator)

You must **not** use a calculator for this paper. Total mark for this paper is 50.
Figures in brackets printed down the right-hand side of pages indicate the marks awarded to each question or part question.
You should have a ruler, compasses, set-square and protractor.

1 (a) Describe fully the transformation which maps shape A onto shape B.

Answer _____

_____ [2]

(b) Enlarge shape A by a scale factor 2, centre (−4, −3) [3]

(c) Rotate shape A by an angle of 90° clockwise about (0, −3) [2]

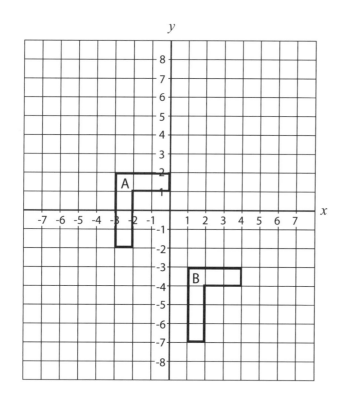

2 Find the value of M when $A = 12$ and $B = -8$

$$M = \frac{6(A - B)}{8}$$

Answer $M = $ _____ [3]

3 Estimate the value of

$$\frac{54.8 \times 4.03}{0.112}$$

Answer _____ [2]

4 Bags of sweets contain between 43 and 47 sweets in total. The probabilities of selecting bags containing each number of sweets are shown in the table below.

No. of sweets	43	44	45	46	47
Probability	0.05	0.15	0.5		0.1

(a) What is the probability of selecting a bag containing 46 sweets?

Answer _____ [2]

(b) What is the probability that a bag contains less than 45 sweets?

Answer _____ [2]

A box contains 500 bags of sweets.
(c) How many bags contain 44 sweets?

Answer _____ [2]

5 (a) Solve the inequality

$3x - 5 > -7$

Answer _____ [2]

(b) Make p the subject of the formula

$5r = 6m + p$

Answer _____ [2]

(c) Simplify

(i) $\dfrac{t^2 \times t^5}{t^3}$

Answer _____ [1]

(ii) $(2x^3y^4) \times (x^4y^2)$

Answer _____ [2]

6 (a) Explain why $2n - 1$ is always an odd number for any positive integer n.

Answer _____

_____ [2]

(b) Hence, by finding the square of $(2n - 1)$, prove that the square of an odd number is always odd.

[2]

7 A five sided spinner has the numbers 1, 2, 3, 4 and 5 labelled on each of its sides. The spinner is spun 500 times. The results are shown in the table below.

Number on spinner	1	2	3	4	5
Frequency	94	105	103	96	102

(a) What is the relative frequency of scoring 3?

Answer _____ [1]

(b) What is the relative frequency of scoring more than 2 on one spin of the spinner?

Answer _____ [2]

(c) Do the results in the table suggest that this is a fair spinner? Give a reason for your answer.

Answer _____

_____ [1]

8 Martha has a fair dice. She throws it twice.
What is the probability that she scores two sixes?

Answer _____ [1]

9 (a) Evaluate $(\sqrt{2})^4$

Answer _____ [1]

(b) Show that
$(\sqrt{8} + \sqrt{18})^2 = 50$

[2]

Maths Revision Booklet T6

10 (a) Which of the following fractions is **not** a recurring decimal?

$$\frac{1}{11} \quad \frac{3}{7} \quad \frac{5}{9} \quad \frac{7}{8} \quad \frac{5}{45}$$

Answer _____ [1]

(b) Change the recurring decimal $0.\dot{8}\dot{1}$ into a fraction.

Answer _____ [2]

(c) Given that $p = \sqrt{8}$, $q = \sqrt{10}$ and $r = \sqrt{5}$, simplify $\frac{pq}{r}$

Answer _____ [2]

11 The letters r, l, d, h and w in all the expressions below represent lengths.
State whether each of the expressions represents a length, area, volume or none of these.

(a) $\pi r^2(r + l)$

Answer _____

(b) $\pi rl + 2d$

Answer _____

(c) $\frac{r\sqrt{(lw^3)}}{h}$

Answer _____

(d) $\frac{(hr^2 + dw^2)}{l^3}$

Answer _____

(e) $\frac{(\pi rlh + 4rw^2)}{rh}$

Answer _____ [3]

12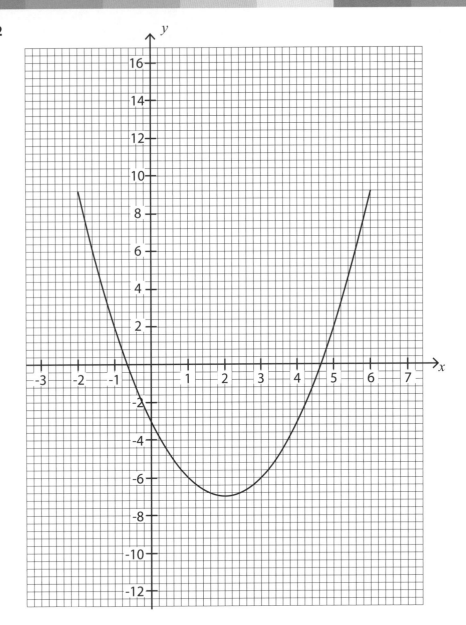

The graph of $y = x^2 - 4x - 3$ for values of x between $x = -2$ and $x = 6$ is drawn above.
By drawing an appropriate linear graph, find the solutions to the equation
$x^2 - 6x + 2 = 0$

Answer $x =$ _____ and $x =$ _____ [2]

13 (a) Complete the table for $y = \frac{-2}{x}$

x	-4	-2.5	-1	1	2	4
$y = \frac{-2}{x}$	$\frac{1}{2}$		2	-2	-1	$-\frac{1}{2}$

[1]

(b) Using the points above, sketch the graph of $y = \frac{-2}{x}$ between $x = -4$ and $x = 4$. Three of the points have already been plotted.

[2]

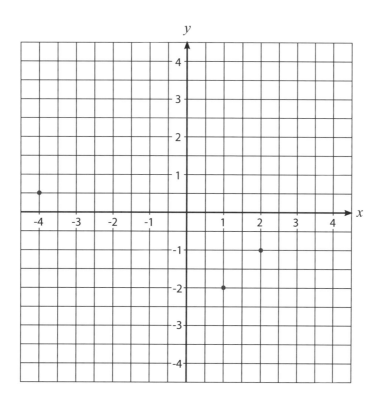

This page has been intentionally left blank.

Revision Exercise 2b (with calculator)

You may use a calculator for this paper. Total mark for this paper is 50.
Figures in brackets printed down the right-hand side of pages indicate the marks awarded to each question or part question.
You should have a ruler, compasses, set-square and protractor.

1

> **SALE!**
>
> 42" PLASMA SCREEN TELEVISION only £599
>
> or Hire Purchase terms: Pay £50 deposit and
> 24 monthly payments at £24.99

Janet decides to pay the sale price for the television as advertised.
How much does she save by not buying the television using Hire Purchase?

Answer £ _____ [2]

2 Prove the identity
$$(2n + 3)^2 - (2n - 3)^2 \equiv 24n$$

Answer _____ [1]

3 Mark bought a computer game on his holidays in the United States. He paid $89.99
Susan bought the same game in Belfast for £34.99
The rate of exchange was £1 = $1.91
Who paid more for their computer game and by how much in pounds and pence?

Answer £ _____ [3]

4 Jill bought a mobile phone and her price package was calculated as follows:
The cost of the line rental is £12.99 per month and calls are charged at 5.4 pence per minute.

(a) Write down a formula for C, the total cost in pounds for her monthly bill, where the length of time for calls is n minutes.

Answer _____ [2]

(b) Calculate Jill's total bill for a month when she had 637 minutes of calls.

Answer £ _____ [1]

(c) Jill's total bill for a particular month is £54.30. Calculate how many minutes of calls she made in this month.

Answer _____ minutes [2]

5

Tanya's back garden is in the shape of a trapezium.
The dimensions of the garden are shown in the diagram above.
The garden is paved apart from a circular pond of radius 3 m in one corner.
What area of the garden is paved?

Answer _____ m² [4]

6

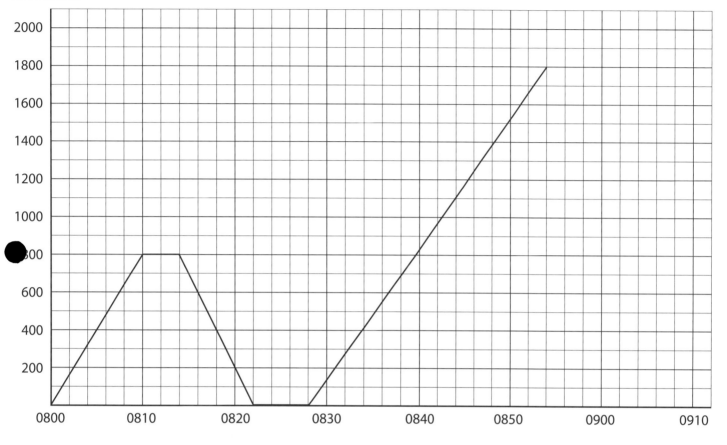

Sushi leaves home at 0800 to cycle to school. At 0810, she stops to buy sweets at the local shop and realises that she has left her money at home. She returns home to collect her money and eventually leaves home again at 0828 and cycles to school. The distance/time graph for her journey is shown above.

(a) How long was Sushi stopped at the shop?

Answer _____ minutes [1]

(b) What was Sushi's average speed in kilometres per hour between home and the shop?

Answer _____ km/hr [2]

Sushi's brother, Alan, leaves home at 0815 and walks to school at a constant speed of 2.4 km/hr.

(c) Draw the line which represents Alan's journey to school. [2]

(d) At what times do Alan and Sushi meet each other on the road?

Answer _____ and _____ [2]

(e) How far are Alan and Sushi from school when Sushi passes Alan?

Answer _____ metres [2]

7 The density of gold is 19300 kg/m³. Calculate the mass, in grams, of 3 cm³ of gold.

Answer _____ g [3]

8 (a)

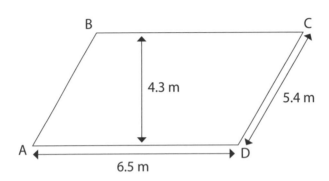

ABCD is a parallelogram with AD = 6.5 m and CD = 5.4 m. The perpendicular distance between the sides BC and AD is 4.3 m.
The parallelogram ABCD forms the base of the prism shown below.
The vertical height of the prism is 5.8 m.

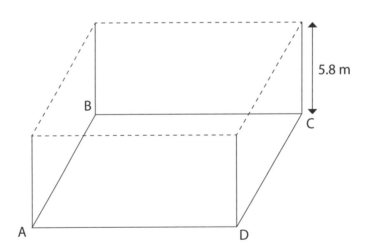

Find the volume of the prism.

Answer _____ [3]

(b) If the dimensions (length, width and height) of the prism are enlarged by a scale factor x, write down an expression for the new volume of the prism.

Answer _____ [1]

9 Given that $L = \sqrt{(m/n)}$, find L in standard form when
$m = 8.1 \times 10^4$ and $n = 3.6 \times 10^8$

Answer _____ [2]

10

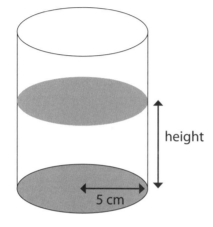

A cylindrical can of base radius 5 cm contains a soft drink. A volume of 125π cm³ of the drink is contained in the can. Find the surface area of liquid in contact with the can in terms of π.

Answer _____ cm² [3]

11 Kristin receives an iPod and a Playstation on his birthday.
The probability that the iPod will develop a fault in the first 3 years is 0.6
The probability that the Playstation will develop a fault in the first 3 years is 0.45

By drawing a tree diagram or otherwise, find the probability that

(a) neither device develops a fault within the first 3 years,

Answer _____ [3]

(b) only one of the devices develops a fault in the first 3 years.

Answer _____ [3]

12 A sheet of cardboard in the form of a sector of a circle of angle 90° and radius 10 cm is folded to form an open conical cup to hold sweets.

10 cm

10 cm

(a) What is the length of the arc of this sector in terms of π ?

Answer _____ cm [2]

(b) Hence find the radius, r, of the base of the open conical cup.

Answer _____ cm [2]

(c) Use Pythagoras' theorem to find the vertical height of the cup.

Answer _____ cm [1]

(d) Hence, find the volume of the cup.

Answer _____ cm³ [2]

ANSWERS

1a (non-calculator)

1

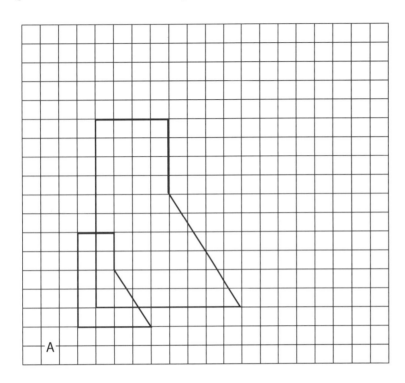

2 (a) −12 **(b)** 97.5

3 20

4 (a) 0.15 **(b)** 0.75 **(c)** 0.4 × 240 = 96

5 (a) a^7 **(b)** $\frac{10}{6}$ or $\frac{5}{3}$ or 1.66 …

6

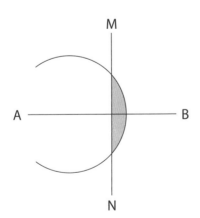

All points less than 7 cm from A are inside the circle, centre A, radius 7 cm. MN is the perpendicular bisector of AB. Hence, the locus is the shaded area as shown.

7 (a) area **(b)** volume

8 (a) 3, −9 **(b)** points plotted, smooth curve (not straight line segments)
  (c) −0.3, 3.3 approx **(d)** $2x^2 - 6x - 5 = -3 \longrightarrow 2x^2 - 6x - 2 = 0$

9 (a) 5 **(b)** 0.363636…. **(c)** $\frac{5\sqrt{3}}{6}$ **(d)** $\frac{\sqrt{3}}{30}$

10 (a) $9x^4y^6z^8$ **(b)** $cxt - cy = s \longrightarrow c(xt - y) = s \longrightarrow c = \frac{s}{(xt-y)}$

  (c) $25 + 20\sqrt{10} + 40 = 65 + 20\sqrt{10}$

11 (a) $\frac{AD}{DE} = \frac{AB}{BC}$ so $\frac{x}{r} = \frac{h}{R}$ hence $x = \frac{rh}{R}$

  (b) $V = \frac{1}{3} \pi R^2 h - \frac{1}{3} \pi r^2 x$

  $V = \frac{1}{3} \pi R^2 h - \frac{1}{3} \pi r^2 \frac{rh}{R}$

  $V = \frac{1}{3} \pi h (R^2 - \frac{r^3}{R}) = \frac{\pi h}{3R}(R^3 - r^3)$

2a (with calculator)

1 (a) Always even, since n^2 is odd as odd × odd = odd
  (b) The sum of the prime number 2 and any other prime number is odd

2 (a) 3 **(b)** 150, 18, 2850

3 31000 − 5435 = 25565
  10% of £2230 = £223
  25565 − 2230 = £23335
  22% of £23335 = £5133.70
  Total tax paid = 5133.70 + 223 = £5356.70

4

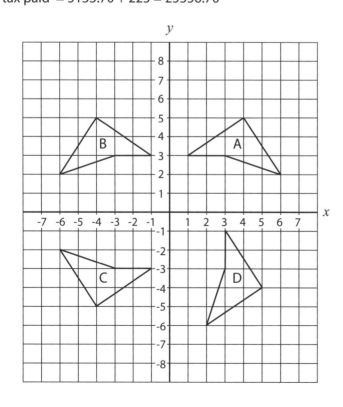

(d) C rotates A through 180° about the origin.

5 (a) 15 min **(b)** 5 **(c)** horizontal line from 12 to 12.40 at 100 miles, line from (12.40, 100) to 2.40pm on horizontal axis **(d)** line from 9.30 through (10.30, 45) and (11.30, 90) **(e)** Readings at 35 and 15 miles giving 20 miles **(f)** 11.10am **(g)** 25

6 998 = 1000 (appropriate degree of accuracy)

7 $\frac{3}{5} \times 200 + \frac{3}{4} \times 300 = 120 + 225 = 345$

8 $(4.902 \times 10^{11}) \div (8.6 \times 10^{6}) = 5.7 \times 10^{4}$

9 (a)

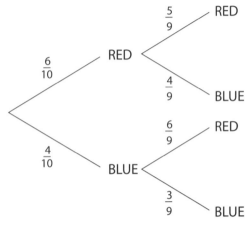

(b) $\frac{4}{10} \times \frac{3}{9} = \frac{12}{90} = \frac{2}{15}$

(c) $1 - \frac{2}{15} = \frac{13}{15}$

10 $\pi r l + \pi r^2 = (360\pi)$ 1131cm²

11 (a) (i) 0.504 **(ii)** 0.006 **(iii)** 1 − 0.006 = 0.994 **(b)** 0.902

1b (non-calculator)

1 (a) Translation $\begin{pmatrix} 4 \\ -5 \end{pmatrix}$

(b) and **(c)**

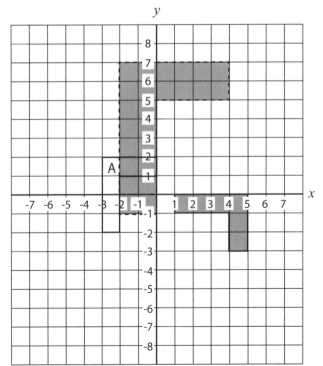

2 15

3 2000

4 (a) 0.2 **(b)** 0.2 **(c)** 0.15 × 500 = 75

5 (a) $x > -\frac{2}{3}$ **(b)** $p = 5r - 6m$ **(c) (i)** t^4 **(ii)** $2x^7y^6$

6 (a) Two times n is always an even number for any positive integer n, so by subtracting 1 we always get an odd number

(b) $(2n - 1)^2 = 4n^2 - 4n + 1$
$4n^2$ is even as 4 multiplied by any integer is even.
Similarly $4n$ is even.
$4n^2 - 4n$ is even as an even number minus an even number is even.
Hence, $4n^2 - 4n + 1$ is odd (by adding 1 to an even number)

7 (a) $\frac{103}{500}$ **(b)** $\frac{301}{500}$ **(c)** Yes, as relative frequencies are nearly all 0.2

8 $\frac{1}{36}$

9 (a) 4 **(b)** $8 + 2\sqrt{144} + 18 = 50$

10 (a) $\frac{7}{8}$ **(b)** $\frac{9}{11}$ **(c)** 4

11 (a) volume **(b)** none **(c)** area **(d)** none **(e)** length

12 $x^2 - 6x + 2 = x^2 - 4x - 3 - 2x + 5$
Hence, $x^2 - 6x + 2 = 0$ can be written
$x^2 - 4x - 3 - 2x + 5 = 0$ or
$x^2 - 4x - 3 = 2x - 5$
Graph of $y = x^2 - 4x - 3$ is shown on diagram.
Draw the graph of $y = 2x - 5$ and find the points of intersection.
$x = 0.35$ and $x = 5.6$ approximately.

13 (a) $\frac{4}{5}$ **(b)** Graph curved shape

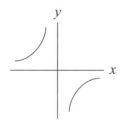

2b (with calculator)

1 24 × 24.99 = 599.76 + 50 = 649.76
Saving = 649.76 − 599 = £50.76

2 $(4n^2 + 6n + 6n + 9) - (4n^2 - 6n - 6n + 9) \equiv 24n$

3 89.99 ÷ 1.91 = £47.11
47.11 − 34.99 = 12.12
Mark paid £12.12 more for his game.

4 (a) $C = 12.99 + 0.054n$ **(b)** £47.39 **(c)** 765 minutes

5 Area of trapezium = $\frac{1}{2}(16 + 23) \times 12 = 234$ m²

Area of pond = $\pi r^2 = \pi (3)^2 = 28.3$ m²

Area of paving = 234 − 28.3 = 205.7 m²

6 (a) 4 min **(b)** 800 m in 10 min = 4800 m in 60 min = 4.8 km/hr **(c)** line from 0815 finishing at (0900, 1800) **(d)** 0820 and 0846 **(e)** 1800 − 1250 (approx) = 550m

7 57.9 grams

8 (a) $V = 6.5 \times 4.3 \times 5.8 = 162.11$ m³ (mark awarded for units m³ here) **(b)** $162.11\, x^3$

9 $L = \sqrt{(2.25 \times 10^{-4})} = 1.5 \times 10^{-2}$

10 $\pi r^2 h = 125\pi$ gives $h = 5$cm

S.A $= \pi r^2$ (base) $+ 2\pi rh$ (curved surface) $= 75\pi$

11 (a) 0.22 **(b)** 0.33 + 0.18 = 0.51

12 (a) $2\pi r \times \dfrac{90}{360} = 2 \times \pi \times \dfrac{10}{4} = 5\pi$ **(b)** $2\pi r = 5\pi$ so $r = 2.5$ cm **(c)** $h = \sqrt{10^2 - 2.5^2} = 9.68$ cm **(d)** 63.36 cm³